THE LIFE AND TIMES OF
TUT-ANKH-AMEN

BY
BISHARA NAHAS

THE BOOK TREE
SAN DIEGO, CALIFORNIA

Originally published 1923
American Library Service
New York

New material, revisions and cover
©2002
The Book Tree
All rights reserved

ISBN 1-58509-087-5

Cover layout and design
Lee Berube

Printed on Acid-Free Paper
in the United States and United Kingdom
by LightningSource, Inc.

Published by
The Book Tree
P O Box 16476
San Diego, CA 92176

We provide fascinating and educational products to help awaken the public to new ideas and information that would not be available otherwise.
Call 1 (800) 700-8733 for our *FREE BOOK TREE CATALOG*.

To
My Father

INTRODUCTION

The famous boy king of Egypt, Tut-Ankh-Amen, was completely unknown to the modern world until his tomb was discovered in the early 20th century by Howard Carter. What Carter found was the first completely untouched and unviolated tomb in the modern world. Most had been found and plundered by treasure-seekers long before the advent of modern archaeology. The incredible gold and riches unearthed with Tut-Ankh-Amen were so amazing that even Carter admitted that he found far more than expected. The gold and jewels associated with this major find have toured the world for years, to the amazement of millions.

It is clear that Tut died while still in his teens. There are those who believe that he was poisoned by priests who wanted his throne due to a difference in religious views. He was buried in about 1350 B.C.

This engaging book provides fascinating information about Tut-Ankh-Amen and ancient Egypt in general. It comes from an author who was himself an Egyptian, and also the former director of several archaeological excavations in Egypt. The depth of his knowledge comes across clearly in this important book, which is both informative and entertaining to read.

Most Westerners must choose from books written by foreign researchers—meaning outsiders from Egyptian culture. This book is an exception. Few other works provide facts from an insider with such knowledge and clarity.

Paul Tice

PREFACE

The eyes of the world astounded by this very old civilization are directed towards Egypt. I have tried in this book to popularize the habits and creeds of the Egyptians under Tut-Ankh-Amen, thus enabling the great mass of the public to be familiar with them. The details, which the monuments have not revealed to us so far, have been supplemented by my knowledge of the actual customs which are the precious inheritance of the past centuries.

BISHARA NAHAS.

Alexandria, Egypt.
Feb. 10, 1923.

CONTENTS

PREFACE

CHAPTER I

                                              PAGE

SHORT HISTORY OF EGYPT 17
    Antiquity of Egypt
      Division by Dynasties
      The first Pharaoh Menas
      The IVth Dynasty, Pyramid builders
        Significance of the Pyramids
        Origin of the Sphynx
      Wider Classification

CHAPTER II

AN EGYPTIAN VILLAGE
    Buildings 27
      Building materials
      Division of the Houses
    Inhabitants
      Men, agriculturists and craftsmen
      Women, their situation in life
      Children
    Furniture
    Ruins

CHAPTER III

EXCAVATIONS IN EGYPT 37
    Napoleon
    Mariette,—the Department of Antiquities
    Popular belief
    Regulations
    Lord Carnarvon and Howard Carter
    Work in excavations

CONTENTS

CHAPTER IV

The Dynasty of Tut-Ankh-Amen 49
    Conquests of the Pharaohs of the XVIII Dynasty
    Their wealth
    Religion of the Egyptians
        Temples—Regligious disposition of the people
        Origin of religion—Monotheism
        Polytheism
    Legend of Osiris
        Power of the Priests of Amen
    Heresy of Akhen-Aton
        Cult of Aton
        Egypt under Akhen-Aton

CHAPTER V

Life of Tut-Ankh-Amen
    He succeeds Akhen-Aton 63
        His name
        His origin
    His life
        His childhood, his studies
        His marriage to the daughter of the Pharaoh
            Marriage ceremony
            Songs
        His house and occupation at Khut-Aton
    Tut-Ankh-Amen ascends to the throne
        Investiture at Thebes
        His wars
        His palace at Thebes and his daily occupations
        His death after a short reign

CHAPTER VI

Significance of the Tomb
    Importance of the tomb 83
        Tomb thieves
        Iconoclasts
    Different forms of tombs
        In old times
        Under the XVIII Dynasty
    Description of Tut-Ankh-Amen tomb
        Its symbolic sculptures and inscriptions

CONTENTS

PAGE

Tomb dwelling of the "Ka"
  What is a "Ka"
  Life of the "Ka"
    material life
    preparations for its sustenance
  Modern habits similar to the old ones

CHAPTER VII

MUMMIFICATION OF TUT-ANKH-AMEN 97
  Sorrow of the population
  Embalming process
    Method used for Tut-Ankh-Amen
    Other methods
  Bandaging
    Papyrus from the Book of the Dead
    Scarabs and amulets

CHAPTER VIII

FUNERAL FESTIVITIES 105
  Festivities in the temple
  Crossing the Nile
  Procession on the West Bank
    Funeral offerings
    Furniture
    Burial

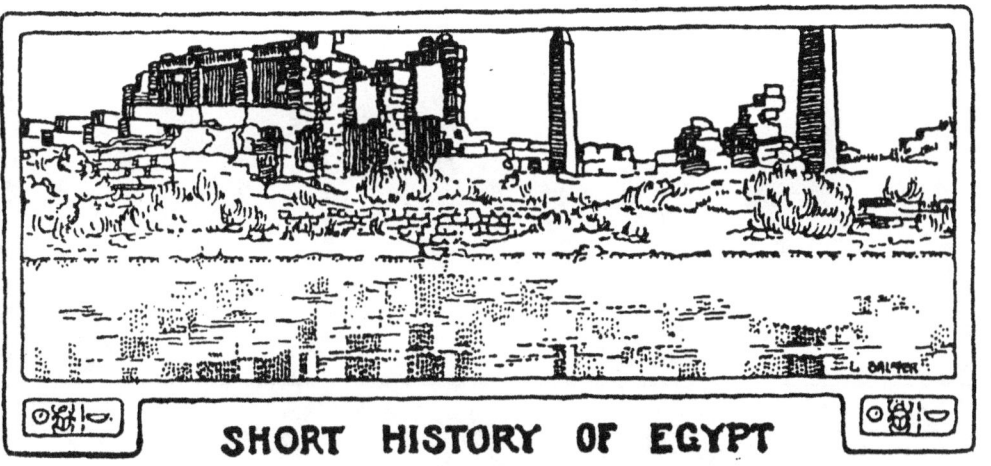

SHORT HISTORY OF EGYPT

CHAPTER I

SHORT HISTORY OF EGYPT

The traveler arriving in Egypt is amazed at the antiquity of her monuments, vestiges of a civilization which have faded, leaving only gigantic ruins, which everyone admires, and eagerly interrogates the mystery of thought and expression concealed in them. The student questioning the constructive idea which conceived these monuments, is fascinated by the secrets they hide. He always finds mention of achievement and supernatural power given to a few chosen persons well versed in the science of magic, but never any explanation of this science comes forth, and he continues his explorations and studies without ever solving the mystery.

Ampere, the famous French scientist of the Nineteenth Century, said jokingly that "A voyage in Egypt was a donkey ride and a boat excursion intermingled with ruins." Perhaps the superficial observer will enjoy only the donkey ride and boat excursion, but the more serious minds of our thinking age are attracted by the symbols of these ruins.

How old are they? How old was this civilization? Questions which have never been definitely answered.

The first reliable historian of Egypt was Manethon, priest of Sebennytos, who lived about 280 B. C. and was ordered by Ptolemey Philadelphus to write a history of Egypt from the beginning of the known ages.

The name of Pharaoh signifies "ruler." It comes from an Egyptian word meaning the "House of Majesty," still found in the Coptic language, which is derived directly from the Egyptian, and is used now only in the Liturgy of the Coptic Church. The popular language spoken in Egypt is Arabic, which has but slight connections with the primitive Egyptian.

Manethon is the first historian who divided the Pharaohs into dynasties, which is a classification of the past rulers by families or by the seat of their empire. The thirtieth dynasty is the one preceding the Ptolemaic one, which started 340 B. C. when the empire built by Alexander the Great was divided between his generals after his death, and Egypt fell to Ptolemy Lagus, Cleopatra being the last of the Ptolemaic Dynasty.

The ancient Egyptians did not use this classification, in fact they had no classification at all.

The valuable works of Manethon are lost, but happily some fragments, including his classification, were kept and quoted by the early historians of the second and third century A. D., as Eusebius, Julius Africanus, and Josephus.

At first his works were believed to be untrue, but later findings have proved that at least in his classification Manethon was correct. A stella found at Abydos represents the Pharaoh Seti I pointing to his son, Rameses II, the names of 76 Pharaohs who had preceded him, and urging him to follow the example set by the mighty and powerful rulers, his predecessors on the throne. Another tablet found at Sakhara by Mariette, and one found at Karnak by Burke, give the names of Pharaohs corresponding to the succession given by Manethon, so does the valuable Papyrus now in the Turin Museum.

Unfortunately these lists are all incomplete and none of them gives any dates. Opinions vary regarding the period of the reigns of each individual Pharaoh. The main basis we have actually for dating the different Pharaohs is the recorded astronomical facts which occurred during their reign, and which can be dated by astronomers.

Manethon, the Abydos stella, the Turin Papyrus, etc., agree that Menas was the first Pharaoh of the first Dynasty. Who was he, and when did he reign? No one knows. It is known that he united the crowns of Upper and Lower Egypt under his sceptre, and moved his capital from This near Abydos to Memphis, now buried under the sands of the desert a few miles south of modern Cairo.

He is also said to have introduced in Memphis the cult of Ptah and erected a temple called "Het-Ptah-ka" or "temple of the genius Ptah." Some say the Greeks derived from it the name of Aegyptos and Copts.

According to Flinders Petrie, Menas reigned about 5500 B. C. According to Brugsh Bey and the Berlin School, Menas' reign started about 4400 B. C., basing their calculations on three generations of Pharaohs to a century. The archaeologists' opinions are divided between these two dates. A general consensus dates, however, around 3400 B. C., the building of the great Pyramid by Khufu, second Pharaoh of the IVth Dynasty. Its construction took place when the constellation Alpha Draconis was visible to anyone who looked up through the slant tunnel on the north side of the Pyramid and helped to find the true north basis of the construction of this Pyramid.

It is proved that Alpha Draconis was visible through this tunnel around 3400 B. C. and before that only during the year 28,500 B. C. The period between 3400 B. C. and 28,500 B. C. was called by Egyptian astronomists, who had studied the movements of the stars, the "great precessional period" during which occurred the formation of Egypt under the direct reign of the Gods.

SHORT HISTORY OF EGYPT

It is interesting to know that the base of the great Pyramid contains 365¼ times the sacred cubit, representing the year, and that the sacred cubit is one twenty-millionth part of the diameter of the earth. Its height is one thousand millionth part of the distance from the earth to the sun. It is placed at 30 degrees of latitude (with an error due to refraction of 1'9"). Its angle gives the coefficient 3.1416 which is used in the calculation of the circumference and the area of a circle. The pyramid builders knew, therefore, that the earth was round, knew the distance to the sun, and the principles of geometry.

We can only regret today that the principles of their science has been lost through the ages, and that it required the genius of Galileus and Copernic 6000 years later to establish these principles of astronomy.

It took 100,000 men twenty years to build the great Pyramid. Lately an account of the rations of corn and onions allowed to the workers has been found. A modern statistician has tried to find out how many bushels of onions expressed in calories would produce the power necessary to raise these masses of stones. I doubt, however, if in our modern times it would be possible to build such a monument with an equal amount of onions consumed.

It certainly took more than a thousand years to attain such a perfect degree of civilization as to be able not only to build huge monuments like the Pyramids, but also to conceive them, and embody in their construction the principles of astronomy and geometry.

The Sphynx is still older than the Pyramids and the Egyptians refer to it as having been carved by the "Hor Heshu" or worshippers of Horus during the reigns of the gods. The priests knew under whose reign the work was done, but unfortunately the tablet placed between the paws of the Sphynx by Thoutmes IV, and supposed to contain its history, has come to us mutilated, and the temple excavated under it does not contain any inscription.

The Sphynx remains to this day a standing mystery of the beginning of art, as the Pyramids are a mystery of science, and in its enigmatic smile baffles the modern utilitarian mind which questions its usefulness.

The origin of this civilization loses itself in the night of time and dates are only a help to place approximately the different known Pharaohs and the periods of their reign.

A wider classification has also been adopted:—

Predynastic Period:—Of which very little is known.

Ancient Empire:—I to XI Dynasties, 5500 to 2000 B. C. Rise of the Empire, called also the Pyramid age. The builders of the three large Pyramids belonged to the IVth Dynasty.

Middle Empire:—XII to XIX Dynasties, 2000 to 1100 B. C. Egypt is at her highest, reaching her greatest period of wealth and power during the XVIIIth and XIXth Dynasties.

Modern Empire:—XX to XXX Dynasties, 1100 to 340 B. C. Decadence. All the provinces and conquests were lost one by one and Egypt fell definitely into the hands of foreign rulers.

AN EGYPTIAN VILLAGE

CHAPTER II

AN EGYPTIAN VILLAGE

Ruins are scattered all over Egypt and there is scarcely a village which has not several "kom" or mounds covering the sites of ancient villages, where centuries before Christ was born, men dwelt, and toiled for sustenance and life in the same manner as they do to-day.

Ages ago dwellings in Egypt were constructed of sun-dried bricks of the same size and pattern as to-day, only temples or mosques being built of stone. An outside wall four feet high encircles a conglomeration of buildings one story high which were composed of the "Harim" or women's dwelling, being the private apartments of the owner where no stranger is permitted to enter, the "dawar," stores, granaries and stables, and the "mandara" or reception room where the owner receives his men friends and transacts his business. The roofs of the houses are made of reeds and beaten mud. Sometimes a primitive open-air stairway leads to one or two light rooms built on the roofs, where the inhabitants can dwell and breathe during the warm nights of the summer.

In the granary is the flour mill made of two revolving stones under which the grain is crushed by turning by hand the upper stone. One of the rooms, which has a circular opening in its middle, forms the kitchen in which a brick oven is constructed; there the bread is baked and the meals are cooked. There are no windows in the buildings to keep them cool in summer and warm in winter. They are occupied only for sleeping quarters, as the life of the population is spent mostly out of doors.

In passing through the villages one can easily imagine himself transported to the past and gazing at the living subjects of the Pharaohs of the Eighteenth Dynasty, whose features have become familiar through the numerous bas-reliefs. The men, tall and wiry, appear in what was originally a loin cloth but is now a long shirt extending midway to their ankles. The garment is dyed dark blue with natural indigo. The laborers can be seen going to work in the fields carrying a flat hoe and bags of seeds on their backs. It is planting time. The Nile has retired to between its banks after having inundated and fertilized the black soil. Long horned cattle are seen slowly plodding their way. Their task is to tread on the soft ground, or drag the light plow made of a beam of wood and a flat iron or wooden

AN EGYPTIAN VILLAGE

share fixed to the beam at an acute angle, and which sinks two or three inches in the ground covering the seed, protecting it from the birds. No plowing or turning of the soil is necessary. The men do not hurry to their work but travel slowly, as they have plenty of time. The day is long in Egypt and no change in temperature is to be expected.

Herodotus declared that the Egyptians were the most lazy and most fortunate people because all of their work was done for them by nature and by their father, the Nile. He said: "As soon as the river had uncovered the ground and the soil was dry enough to support their feet, they would go and scatter the seed broadcast, bring their large herds of cattle to trample on the grain and cover it. After that, they patiently waited for the crop to grow and mature, which was done without the help of any rain or irrigation, the humidity of the soil being sufficient to feed the growing crop. When the time of harvest would come they would bring the crop to their yard where the cattle would tread on the ears and separate the grain from the straw." No unexpected misfortunes had to be contended with, and the crop was sure to be ripe in time owing to the beneficency of the Nile. Is it any wonder that the Nile was worshipped and believed to be the maker and father of Egypt? Some pretend that he was Osiris lying dead in his coffin, representing the river banks, and resurrecting regularly to fertilize the soil of the country.

The craftsmen of Egypt go about their work with the same tools as of old, the carpenter with a lathe operated by his feet, the potter and his clay, selling the porous jars, "goullas," which keep the water cool in summer, and repairing the broken pottery, the dyer with his hand stained blue from the indigo he uses, and the mason with his hammer and trowel.

The women gather in the streets and talk about the latest news or scandal. They wear loose garments, usually black. Their hair is tightly fixed under a cape and is carefully separated into a large number of long plaits with fringes at the ends. According to their wealth or station in life, they wear decorated pectorals and necklaces made of gold, silver or amber beads. They also wear bracelets and armlets of colored glass, rings of crystal and semi-precious stones curiously carved, and silver anklets, which make a metallic sound when they walk. Their eyes are beautified by the addition of a black line on the eye-brows, and the eye-lids are painted with "kohl," a mixture of antimony, which make them look darker. They go about their daily work covered with their jewelry, which they never take off. At sunset they can be seen going to the river for water, carrying large pots which they gracefully balance on their heads.

The women of Egypt marry when they are about twelve years old. Contrary to the common belief of those who do not know the intimate life of the Oriental, they enjoy great freedom. The woman rules her house, goes freely about the village and to the market to dispose of the farm products. In spite of the easy divorce habits of the Egyptian, the position of the wife is secure when she is the mother of children, over whom she has complete authority until they become of age. She is called then the "nanern," the "lady of the house." If she is divorced the law gives her a dowry, alimony and charge of the children. The greatest respect is paid her. The Precepts of Ptah-Hotep, written about 3,200 B. C., declare: "If thou wouldst be a wise man, love thy wife wholly and constantly. Feed her and clothe her, love her tenderly, and fulfil her desires as long as thou livest, for she is an estate which conferreth great reward upon her lord. Be not hard to her, for she will be more easily moved by persuasion than by force."

Individual names in Egypt always have a meaning and to the girls pet names are given. They are called "Sweet" or "Little Cat" or "Pearl of the Eye" or "Milk of Dawn" or "Honey."

The children, scantily dressed, run about and until they can walk are never left alone, their mother carrying them on her back or shoulders. As soon as they can walk they are taught to be useful. They take the cows to the pasture along the banks of the Nile and the canals, they gather the fodder and weeds for the food of the cattle, the material for the fire, usually sun dried dung, millet stalks and branches of trees.

The similarity of the modern people to their ancestors is so great that one would expect, if one can wait long enough, to see the herald coming and announcing to the "cheikh-el-beled" or chief of the village that the Pharaoh Saaka-Ra and his wife, the eldest daughter of Akhen-Aton, had been deposed through the influence of the priests of Amen, and that Tut-Ankh-Amen and his wife Ankh-Sen-Amen, the second daughter of Akhen-Aton, have been elevated to the throne, because they were expected to renounce the faith of the heretic king and return to the worship of Amen, the god of their fathers.

Perhaps the outward expression of life, the beliefs and forms of government change, but the fundamental customs and habits have remained the same throughout the ages.

The houses have not much furniture, which is principally found in the temples, palaces and villas of the nobles. The Egyptians sleep on the floor on a reed mat to protect them from the dampness of the ground; they usually sit in a squatting position or on their feet. They have no table to eat on. The food is brought on trays which are placed on the floor and around which the family gathers. Their clothes, few in number, and the women's toilet articles such as mirrors, cosmetics, bottles and unguent vases, are in a wooden chest. Along the walls of the reception room a high seat is built of mud, on which the guests can sit.

With a few rains these dried mud brick houses become one solid mass, and when after a few years any portion crumbles down, it is immediately rebuilt without taking care to even clear away the debris, which is used to make the floor of the new house. No foundation is ever laid and it is cheaper to rebuild a new house on the older one than clear the fallen remains. Little by little the villages become higher and higher until they stand on an eminence over the plain surrounding them. This is a good thing because they are not covered by the water from the inundations of the Nile, which transforms them during three months of the year into miniature islands in a bush of palm trees.

Modern villages are constructed on older ones and it is not uncommon to find several superposed layers belonging to different periods of the history of Egypt, and in which remains of pottery, cooking utensils, scarabs and cheap jewelry are found.

The cultivated area of Egypt was at one time much larger than it is now. About 12,000,000 acres were in production under the New Empire, whereas now barely 7,000,000 acres of land are under cultivation. Egypt was called the "Granary of the World" under the Roman Empire, and used to export regularly to Rome an enormous quantity of grain. Now we have to import part of our wheat and flour for our subsistence, although the number of inhabitants is not larger than it was before the Christian era. The neglect into which the canals and irrigation works had fallen under the Byzantine, Arab and Turkish empires is the cause of such a reduction in the cultivated era. It is due to the vigorous progressive attitude taken by the actual reigning family from its founder, the Glorious Mohamed-Ali, that Egypt has regained part of her prosperity.

The villages covering the abandoned area fell in ruins and were deserted. They form "koms" or mounds, which the cultivators use as manure because of their high contents in organic matter and nitrogen.

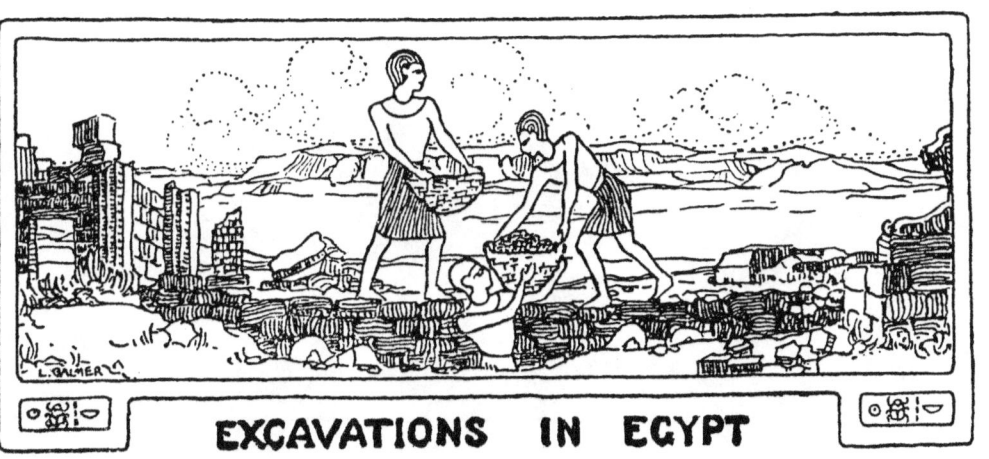
EXCAVATIONS IN EGYPT

CHAPTER III

EXCAVATIONS IN EGYPT

The first attempt to study Egyptian monuments was made by Napoleon during his campaign of Egypt at the beginning of the Nineteenth Century. He was accompanied by a staff of archaeologists, but the net result of their efforts to penetrate the mysteries of the land they had invaded, merely consisted of a number of sketches and a classification of the ruins, as known to the natives of that period, because they were unable to read the inscriptions on the monuments.

Among their discoveries was the famous Rosetta Stone, now in the British Museum and which served to decipher the hieroglyphic and demotic languages. It is a trilingual stella, on which the same text was written in three languages:—Greek, demotic and hieroglyphic. Young first tried, and Champollion succeeded in deciphering the inscriptions by comparing them with the Greek, and thus started the hieroglyphic alphabet.

During the first part of the Nineteenth Century

there were no regulations in Egypt governing excavations, and any one could engage in this work at his own expense on public property and dispose of his discoveries in any manner he desired. As the result of such a situation many valuable objects have been scattered and ruined.

The honor of starting the first Service of Antiquities in Egypt belongs to A. Mariette, a Frenchman, who was commissioned by the Louvre Museum to engage in explorations in the interest of science and for the purpose of securing antiquities for its galleries. He became so interested in his work that he persuaded the Khedive of Egypt, Ismail, to establish a Service of Antiquities, of which he became the first head. He was not given a free hand, however, and in his "Memoirs," complains of the difficulties he encountered, of the smallness of his budget and the impossibility of preventing the smuggling of antiquities.

Later the Service was organized on a better basis and several laws and regulations were introduced. No excavating was allowed on public ground without a special permit and all treasures found were to be delivered to the government, which claimed the sole possession of underground wealth. Whatever was found, however, it shared equally with the discoverer.

Very often discoveries have been made by the natives in digging under their houses or in the koms, and there is no country in the world where the population believes in buried treasure as do the Egyptians. The real caches which have been found add to the natural inclination of the people towards the supernatural, leading them to believe that there are numerous treasures hidden and protected by genii. If the word of magic mastering the guardian of the treasure could be found, and properly pronounced in time, the treasure would become the property of who would say the correct word. It is a case of finding the "Open Sesame" of Ali-Baba to become the owner of incalculable riches.

All around Luxor the popular belief is in mysterious tombs, and the most ignorant "fellah" will speak of the marvelous boat of the sun, made of gold and whose ropes are of silver, which floats on particular nights on the sacred lake, and which no one can see without becoming blind. A learned scholar, Ahmed Pacha Zeki, has gathered in a book the popular belief in treasures scattered all over Egypt, and yet particular to each village. And there are thousands of them.

I believe there is something true in these tales, else how would these ignorant people have known anything about the gold boat of the sun if its story had not been popularly told from father to son for generations.

The Egyptian Government has now forbidden all excavation work without permission but it grants it willingly to anyone qualified and on the express condition that all that is found shall be shared equally with the Cairo Museum, except in the case of an unviolated tomb of a Pharaoh, which would become the property of the Egyptian Government. This is fair enough since the land actually belongs to the Egyptian Government.

In 1894, when Mr. de Morgan was Director of Antiquities, he tried to introduce a new scheme of work. His plan was to have the Cairo Museum in charge of all excavating work which would be carried on actively in all known parts of the country. The unique pieces found would be displayed in the Museum, and all the others, as well as the replica and duplicates already in its possession, would be catalogued and priced. Copies of the catalogues would be sent to the foreign museums and private collectors, who would use the budget devoted to their excavation work in buying the pieces they needed or preferred.

The result of such sales would be applied to further excavation work, without any idea of profit. The foreign collectors could then use their money in buying what they really needed and not blindly excavating without sometimes any result at all.

This scheme did not find favor, as the foreign museums preferred the gamble and excitement attached to their excavation work, and it created marked opposition from the real and pseudo antiquity dealers, who would have found themselves in direct competition with the Cairo Museum.

It is to be regretted that this scheme failed as it would have avoided much complication and smuggling of which high officials of important museums boast. It would also have centralized the work and made it much more comprehensive. The actual system has been in practice for many years and all large museums have their own staff working every winter. I do not know of anyone who can complain of the results of their excavations.

The work done by the excavators has been splendid and has brought to life many unknown facts of ancient Egypt. The Metropolitan Museum of New York has been at work now for the past seventeen years and has a most complete collection from the Predynastic period to the Christian era. Last year under the very able direction of A. M. Lythgoe, the Museum was carrying on work in four different places, and among their most valuable discoveries are the new royal tomb chambers in the Valley of the Kings, the clearing of the Pyramid of Amenemhat I at Lisht, and the palace of Amen-Hotep III at Thebes.

Lord Carnarvon has been working for several

years before finding the tomb of Tut-Ankh-Amen. The story is told of his going one day to the British Museum and asking the trustees what would be the best thing for him to do as he intended to use part of his large income to foster science, and they directed him towards excavation work in Egypt.

He associated with him Mr. Howard Carter, who had been Inspector of Antiquities of Upper Egypt under the most able G. Maspero, and who was best designated for it on account of his perfect knowledge of the country and its antiquities. I remember meeting Mr. Carter four years ago during our passage on the S. S. Helouan from Alexandria to Trieste. He is a most modest man, speaking reluctantly of his work, but most fascinating when in the presence of someone interested. He charmed the long hours of the journey by his tales.

With untiring tenacity he stuck to the clearing of one particular point in the Valley of the Kings, where his knowledge of the habits of old Egyptians convinced him that he could find the burial place of one of the Pharaohs. When the patience of Lord Carnarvon was near an end, he was enthusiastic and persuaded his wealthy backer to continue the excavations.

Mr. Carter proceeded systematically in his work. He installed a small narrow gauge railroad line to remove all the debris and dirt to a spot distant enough not to encumber his future works. I can imagine his moments of suspense when he found the sealed door on which the designs indicated a tomb, and his feeling of anticipation before its opening.

He acknowledges that he found much more than he expected to. This is a case where realizations surpassed expectations.

The importance of this tomb is that it is the first tomb of a Pharaoh which has been found unviolated and in it the deceased resting with all his surroundings as he was buried by the priests in 1,350 B. C.

From 1908 until 1915 I directed excavation work in different parts of Egypt and spent several winters in Upper Egypt where I had many opportunities of visiting the Valley of the Kings.

The work is done now in the same way and with the same implements as thousands of years ago. Men under the supervision of an overseer or "kholi" to each twenty-five men, dig with the flat shoed hoe and fill baskets of palm leaf, having a capacity of about thirty pounds of earth; boys and young men take from the diggers the filled baskets and in a long string carry them on their shoulders to a spot where they empty them, whether it is in a railroad car or on a dump-heap. They return with their empty baskets which they throw at the feet of the diggers and take a full one. These baskets are easily broken and torn, but they are immediately replaced as they cost only two or three cents a piece. The work goes on like that from sunrise to sunset with one hour for lunch and rest, lunch taken on the spot and consisting generally of some corn bread and an onion, which the men bring with them. The fresh and sweet water of the Nile refreshes them.

It is astonishing the amount of work which is done during a day by a gang of ten diggers and twenty carriers, paid from twenty to forty cents a day.

To make the work less monotonous and tedious, a man usually sings a popular song and all the laborers sing the verse in chorus, digging or walking with the rhythm of the music, as Egyptians are naturally musical. These songs refer to a sweetheart left behind, or to the marvelous exploits of a young man in love with an unknown girl whom he has seen once; sometimes when an important personage comes to visit the place, the singer improvises a verse in his honor, and a nickname is given to the visitor if his name is not known or difficult to pronounce, and if the visitor does not understand the language. Egyptians are very witty and prone to laugh at small matters.

If large stones have to be transported they are pulled on sledges or tied with ropes and rolled on trunks of palm trees while the men draw on the ropes. The inclined plan is used to raise or lower them and a causeway is prepared in front of them.

No complicated devices of machinery, lever and pulleys. What is the use of these complications? Labor is so cheap, and the bas-reliefs of the temples have taught them how their fathers worked before them. Labor was still cheaper then, as the workmen had only to be fed, and probably did not receive any salary.

Excavations have to be very carefully supervised. Besides the different overseers, a faithful director must be present at all times while the excavating is done, and must control with scrutiny the diggers who are prompt to hide a piece of jewelry, a scarab which they might find. The temptation is so great, and the salary is so small! An agent of the Department of Antiquities is also usually present and mails to Cairo daily report of the work done.

CHAPTER IV

THE DYNASTY OF TUT-ANKH-AMEN

The XVIII Dynasty, of which Tut-Ankh-Amen is one of the last rulers, marks precisely the most prosperous period of the Middle Empire, and the Pharaohs of this dynasty reigned from 1580 B. C. to 1325 B. C., the undisturbed rulers of the entire country.

The first Pharaoh of the XVIII Dynasty was Aahmes I, who liberated his country from the yoke of the foreign rulers, the Hyksos, who had established themselves in Lower Egypt. He drove them out and again united Egypt under one rule. He was a mighty soldier and great fighter and was forced to engage in several sharply fought battles with the Hyksos and their followers before driving them out. In his tomb was found the body of one of the princes who had fallen probably on the battlefield, having still traces of heavy wounds inflicted upon him during battle.

The Pharaohs of the XVIII Dynasty enlarged the domain of Egypt, leading the victorious armies east as far as the Euphrates, conquering in the north the kingdom of the Hittites and the Syrian kings, and going far south to punish the Kings of Ethiopia.

Thotmes III, who reigned 53 years (of which 22 as co-regent with his sister Hatschepaut), was one of the greatest conquerors. During the 31 years of his reign alone, he invaded Syria and Babylonia seventeen times. He spent the winters in Thebes, and went north during the summer when the heat became unbearable. His idea of a summer vacation was to invade the northern countries.

On the pylon of the temple of Karnak, he recorded the names of 360 towns which he conquered, and which paid tribute to him.

All the newly conquered people were obliged to pay a yearly tribute to the Pharaoh, who became thus immensely wealthy, receiving from the East annual tributes of brass, silver, lead, precious woods, cattle and horses, and from the South, gold or electron, ivory, precious stones and slaves. These tributes were delivered regularly to the Egyptian treasury, and with pleasure, as mentioned in a letter written by the Governor of Sydon:—"To the King, my Lord, my God, my Sun, giving my Lord, this is said:—I, Khazanou of the city, thy servant, dust of thy feet and ground on which thou treadest, the seat of thy chair, hoof of thy horse, I roll on my stomach and on my back seven times in the dust at the feet of my King, of my Lord, son of Heaven. The city of Sydon, the slave of the King, my Lord, as entrusted to me is quiet. On reading the order of the King, my Lord, my heart leapt with joy, I raised my head; my face and my eyes were beaming when I transmitted to my people the order of the King, my Lord . . . thus: Thy servant sends thee 100 oxen and also female slaves. News for the King, my Lord, Son of the Heaven."

The Pharaohs indeed were extremely rich. Abyssinia, the mines of Ethbaye, Sinai, and the Red Sea Islands supplied them profusely with washed gold, native gold, emerald turquoises and semi-precious stones. A proverb then alluded to by the Kings of Asia said: "In Egypt gold is as plentiful as dust in lavish supply. . . . The dust of roads is in that country pure gold." One of their vassals holding for them a far away country wrote to the Pharaoh, "Send me gold. . . . I am going to send for thy gold . . . formerly thy father sent to my father much gold. Thou shouldest send me the same quantity of gold thy father sent."

During the XVIII Dynasty the horse made its first appearance in Egypt, where it was used in drawing the battle chariots. It seems that Egyptians became familiar with it during their Asiatic campaigns, and imported it from the conquered people in whose annual tribute horses were included.

Like many great conquerors, the Pharaohs of the XVIII Dynasty were great builders, and everywhere in Egypt traces of their temples can be seen. Their most important work being the completion of the temples of Amon and of Mut at Luxor and Karnak, and the mortuary temples of Deir-El-Bahari and Medinet-Habout at Thebes. The modern name of Luxor means "The Palaces." They also built for themselves, hewn in the rock, tombs which they expected to be eternal, in the part known actually as the "Valley of the Kings."

All over Egypt in Nubia, in Syria, they either completed, or constructed new temples. The buildings are not all of the same age, but have been added to or rebuilt from the foundations to replace older ones which had fallen into decay. Very few traces are found of the original buildings, and they can be compared to that "Bill" which after passing through the hands of many committees had been so changed, that only the word "whereas" remained from the original.

Their activity was mostly directed towards the building of temples to satisfy the religious disposition of the people. Herodotus said that the Egyptians were the most religious people in the world and devoted all their life to the worship of gods and to prepare themselves for a future life.

Religion, which, as in all primitive civilization, had started by monotheism, had degenerated, and the attributes of the gods were worshipped instead of the god himself, thus creating polytheism.

The initiated priests, who had been taught the principles of this religion, believed in only one deity who was the "Creator," the "Almighty," "who is and was and will be," and whose name was never mentioned. They understood the multiple powers of the Supreme Being, but they did not impart this knowledge to the common people. Sir G. W. Wilkinson says in "Manners and Customs of Ancient Egyptians," Vol. 1: "It was unjust and inconsistent that the priesthood should have a creed peculiar to themselves, and the people be left in utter ignorance of the fundamental doctrines of their religion; that in proportion as their ideas were raised toward the contemplation of the nature of a God, the other classes, tyrannically forbidden to participate in those exalted studies, should be degraded by a belief totally at variance with the truths imparted to the initiated, and whilst these last were acquainted with the existence of one Deity in Unity and the operations of the creative power, that the uninstructed should be left and even taught to worship a multiplicity of Deities, whose only claims to adoration were grounded upon fable."

This multiplicity of forms of worship was,

however, rational and based on serious grounds as Plutarch said in "De Iside": "It is evident that the religious rites and ceremonies of the Egyptians were never instituted on irrational grounds or built on mere fables and superstitions. All was founded with a view of promoting the morality and happiness of those whose solemn duty it was to observe them."

The different Gods were only manifestations of the Creator in his principal attributes. They were represented by an emblem, symbolic of their activity. The people were taught to believe in the real sanctity of the emblematic idol, until the idol was confused with the attribute itself and worshipped in its material form, as modern superstitious people venerate relics with the same devotion as the person from whom these relics come.

A good example is the legend of Osiris who was the god presiding on the Underworld life of the Egyptian after his death. Osiris was supposed to have descended on earth to reign with his wife-sister Isis. His brother Set, the God of Evil, jealous of him, prepared a casket exactly fitting his body. He invited his brother to a great banquet where, after drinking, every one present was challenged to try to lie in the casket. When Osiris tried, the lid of the casket was nailed and he was thrown into the Nile.

Isis informed, wept over her slain husband,

and started a search for his remains. She found a limb in every corner of Egypt, and she buried it on the spot where found. In answer to her prayers to Phtah, the father of the Gods, she had from her deceased husband a son named Horus, whom she sent to avenge her father. Horus has ever since been fighting with his uncle Set, being alternately victorious and defeated.

This legend has its origin from the Nile which periodically covers all Egypt during three months of the year, fertilizing the soil represented by Isis, and returns to its banks represented by the casket. Horus is a personification of the crops grown on the land after the innundation, and the scattered limbs of Osiris are the canals which cover the country, bringing to the most remote parts the fecundating water of the river. The eternal fight between Horus and Set and their alternate victory were the image of the periodical rise of the water, when Set was powerless to prevent Osiris from flooding the country.

The Egyptians adored the Nile, because in it they saw the principle of their prosperity. They also adored the Sun from which the Nile started.

Osiris became the God of the Underworld because the Egyptians believed in an after life where the land was always green and where they could enjoy without interruption, the pleasures of life.

This was the principle of their religion, which degenerated later through ignorance.

Each important town had its main god to whom a temple was erected and who was particularly worshipped, while any other god might also be worshipped at the same time. The most important god in Thebes was Amen to whom beautiful temples at Luxor and Karnak were erected. He had become associated with the Sun God and was known as Amen-Ra, "the creator of all gods and Lord of the throne of the earth." His temple of colossal dimensions extended to the Nile by a double alley of ram-headed sphinxes.

The priests of Amen grew very wealthy and powerful. Their riches came from the endowment of land and revenues bestowed upon them by the successive Pharaohs for the upkeep of the temple and of the Pharaohs' tombs, as we will see later. Thoutmes III merged the priesthood of all the temples of Egypt into one great sacerdotal organization at the head of which he placed the High Priest of Amen, who also became his Grand Vizier, or Prime Minister.

Their power became so great that the Pharaoh Amenhotep IV tried to shake it and to free himself from their influence. This Pharaoh, the predecessor of Tut-Ankh-Amen, reigned from 1377 B. C. to 1358 B. C. and is known as the "Heretic Pharaoh." He owed his ideas of independence mostly to his mother, Queen Thyi, and his wife, Queen Nefertiti, who were princesses of Mitani of northern Syria. They probably taught him the monotheistic idea which they brought from the Asiatic lands and which Ahmenhotep IV tried to impose upon Egypt. As he could not shake the power of Amen and his priests in Thebes, he withdrew from this town after a short period and built between Thebes and Memphis at 180 miles from modern Cairo, the new city of Khut-Aton, the "Horizon of Aton," the ruins of which are called Tell-El-Amarna. He also changed his name from Amenhotep IV, which means "Amen Rests," into Akhen-Aton, which means "The Splendor of Aton." Temples in honor of "Aton" were built by him in other parts of the empire in Abyssinia and in Syria.

Whereas Amen-Ra, representing the Sun, was the most powerful God, he was not the only one, but the most important one in the polytheistic system of religion. Aton, on the other hand, the God of the new Religion, was the only God representing the principle of monotheism. Aken-Aton, whenever he could, on the public buildings, erased the plural of the word "Gods" and replaced it by its singular form.

I do not agree with some modern archeologists who say that Aton representing "The Disk of the Sun" was worshipped as such, but in my opinion, this was only a concrete representation of the abstract idea of God, the Creator of the Universe, and the Bestower of all good. He is represented by the disk of the sun whose radiating beams diverge downward, each ray terminating in a human hand opened in the sublime act of giving. Believing today that this new worship was the worship of the Sun's Disk itself would be as if 3000 years from now, and in case of a great cataclysm in which all our books would be lost, future archaeologists would say that Christians of the nineteenth century worshipped an old man, because God is represented sometimes by such statues in churches, and that the pig was a sacred animal to them because St. Anthony is always represented in the desert in the company of this animal. I object against hasty explanations, and defining as paganism, a religion which is not fully understood.

The foundation of the so-called Akhen-Aton Heresy is the revolt of a broad-minded Pharaoh against polytheism prevailing during his time and his return to the monotheistic idea. Akhen-Aton worshipped the essence of God himself, and represented Him on monuments under His tangible manifestation of Sun giving life. The Aton idea may have originated from the idea of Jehovah of the Hebrews, with whom the Pharaohs were then in close contact. The beautiful hymn addressed to Aton and said to be composed by Akhen-Aton himself, is all impregnated with this idea of the One Creator and would be in its proper place in the Bible.

Akhen-Aton was a reformer and a poet, not a

conqueror. He neglected the conquests of his predecessors. In the tablets of Tell-El-Amarna, which were brick tablets with cuneiform characters used internationally at the time, we find several supplications from the governors of far away provinces asking the Pharaoh for assistance to repel foreign invaders. These demands seem never to have been answered, as one by one, the different provinces held by Egypt were lost. Akhen-Aton proved to be an idealistic poet to whom justice had been denied, as he is commonly called the "Heretic Pharaoh," even by those who ought to defend his ideas of reform.

He did not make any change in the outward expression of Egyptian worship and continued to believe in the same future life. Art, however, during his reign became more realistic under Asiatic influence, and represented for the first time men and animals as they were really seen. These innovations in art were felt under the following Pharaohs even after the complete disappearance of the Aton cult.

LIFE OF TUT-ANKH-AMEN

CHAPTER V

LIFE OF TUT-ANKH-AMEN

Akhen-Aton died at the early age of 34, worn out probably by the struggle he carried on against the powerful Amen priests. He left only daughters; but in Egypt hereditary privileges were transmitted through women as well as men, and he was succeeded on the throne by his eldest daughter, who reigned with her husband Saaka-Ra. Their reign was very brief. They disappeared without leaving any trace and were succeeded by Aken-Aton's second daughter and her husband Tut-Ankh-Amen.

The question very often has been asked how to pronounce Tut-Ankh-Amen. This name is composed of three different words united in one; "Tut" which means "Image"; "Ankh" which means "Life" or "Living," and the name of the God "Amen." Therefore, it ought to be pronounced as three different names united together: "Tut-Ankh-Amen." Opinions also vary regarding the pronunciation of the name of the god "Amen." It is a mistake to pronounce it like the religious word "Amen," commonly used in the Christian prayers, as they are entirely different. The old Egyptians, as well as the modern Egyptians, in their Arabic, did not use vowels in their words, and the latter have the word "Amen" for the prayer, and mention the god as "Amman," which is the correct pronunciation. Therefore, the Pharaoh ought to be called "Tut-Ankh-Amman" insisting on each syllable. I have used the orthograph Tut-Ankh-Amen because it is the usual and adopted one.

Some historians state that Tut-Ankh-Amen was the brother of Akhen-Aton, basing their assertion on the fact that in a monument he referred to Amenhotep III as being his father, and glorified his ascension to his parent's throne. He would have thus married his niece, the daughter of Akhen-Aton, which was quite proper at the time, because to insure in their mind purity of blood, marriages between brother and sister were usual when the sister was the heiress of the throne. Cleopatra married her two brothers one after the other, and the scandal mongers of the time declared she killed both, one after the other.

The new discovery has thrown a great light on Tut-Ankh-Amen, and has given us a greater insight on his intimate life. Little was known about him because his reign was of a very short duration, and his successor Horem-Heb had erased wherever he could, the cartouche of Tut-Ankh-

Amen to replace it by his own (cartouche means cartridge in French, and was first used by Champollion to denominate the oblong seal in which the name of the Pharaoh was inscribed in hieroglyphic. The word "cartouche" has become usual in Egyptology for the name of a God or King in the seal).

A short history of his life will give us a glimpse of the customs of the Pharaohs under the XVIII Dynasty. It will, alas, be only a glimpse, as many details are still unknown. I will describe his life as imagined by a modern Egyptian, basing my practical knowledge on the monuments and remains just found and my speculations on the customs which the inhabitants have preserved through centuries in spite of the changes of religion and forms of government.

Whether he was the son of Amenhotep III or not, it is certain that Tut-Ankh-Amen was of royal blood and descended from a very old family. He came very young to Khut-Aton with Akhen-Aton, when the latter transferred his capital from Thebes, and his name was then Tut-Ankh-Aton.

He spent his youth, as all the boys of noblemen, under the supervision of the women of the "harim," running around as he liked, scantily dressed, the head clean shaven except for a lock of hair left on the top of his head.

Being of royal blood the menial work of following the cattle, and gathering fuel was spared to him, and when he was about five years old, he started to study. He did not go, however, to a public school, but the scribes and priests of the temple came to teach him writing and reading.

He was taught the two forms of writing, the hieroglyphic and hieratic. The first being the idealistic language preserved to us on the monuments, where each word was represented by a figure or a number of figures evocated by the sounds or the property of the word; the hieratic writing is the one used on papyri, accounts and reports, and is a cursive phonetic writing derived from the hieroglyphic but more simplified.

In studying writing he was already acquiring a certain power, as writing being the language of the Gods, a great respect was paid to those who could write. He exercised on a whitewashed hard wood board with a reed pen which he dipped in a thick black paste. The board was daily whitewashed by the servants, and is used today by little Egyptians going to the "kuttabs" or primary schools.

Later on he was taught by the priests the elements of religion, the creation by the gods, their fights, the principles of morality as set in the old books of precepts published by Ptah-Hotep, to be able to live the life of an upright and straightforward man, obedient to the king, respectful of the old beliefs, useful to his fellow-countrymen. He memorized the Books of the Dead and learned

LIFE OF TUT-ANKH-AMEN

the words used to subjugate the evil spirits, and master the elements. After that came the study of magics, medicine, anatomy, astronomy, astrology and arithmetics. Being of royal blood, Tut-Ankh-Aton was destined to a high post in the army or in the priesthood. His education was, therefore, most complete, and the most learned men of the time acted as his tutors.

All this knowledge had to be acquired before he was twelve or thirteen years old, as it was the time set for his marriage with Ankhsen-Aton, the third daughter of Akhen-Aton to whom he had been betrothed since his childhood. Egyptians marry very young and often before reaching the age of puberty; twelve years is not an uncommon age to marry.

The eldest daughter of Akhen-Aton died when still young, his second daughter married Saaka-Ra, who was to succeed him on the throne, and the third one married Tut-Ankh-Aton.

If divorce is easy in Egypt, marriage is easier, and no traces on the monuments are left of any marriage ceremony. It was done as today by a contract registered by the public scribe, signed by both parties and the husband engaged himself to provide for his wife, clothe her, feed her, and treat her gently. Private quarters were provided for her to avoid meeting and mixing with her husband's friends.

A certain dowry was paid by the bridegroom,

wherefrom the idea generalized in the foreign countries that Egyptians buy their wives, when they simply pay to the father a dowry which will revert to the wife in case of divorce. It is a misconstruction of a perfectly good habit, and interpretation of a dowry as a purchase price.

Although the marriage ceremonies are not reproduced on the monuments, an account of them has been faithfully rendered in some papyri and they resemble the ceremonies held in our times. The bride was first anointed with perfumed unguents by her servants and companions, her nails stained with "henna," her eyes blackened with kohl, and her hair arranged in numerous braids. After these preparations she was led in pomp to the house of the bridegroom where the contract was signed.

Egyptians always liked pageants and a long procession preceded by musicians and singers started. Ankhsen-Aton accompanied by her mother and sisters sat on a platform prepared for her on the back of a camel and covered with a tent made of gold braided red linen. The women relatives and friends, her companions in the temples where she had held the position of singer of the God since childhood, followed on camel or donkey back. All the furniture, the utensils of the house, the presents and offerings carried on donkey back or on the heads of men formed the rest of the procession. Here were some of the furniture which will be stored later in the tomb: the beautiful throne, with an Aton design, the disk of the Sun from which the beneficent beams radiated, the features of the young couple were carved on it and inlaid with semi-precious stones; then came the smaller chairs and folding stools, here also was the Hothor couch, which will be the nuptial couch and on which symbolical designs were represented, the pillows "urs" on which Egyptians rest their heads not to disturb the arrangement of their coiffure, the ostrich feather fans which the slaves will agitate to cool the atmosphere during the hot hours of the day, the chests full of the rich robes of the finest linen, plaited or striped and almost transparent. Wool was not used because of the belief that it was impure.

Then came the finely carved bottles and vases full of unguents, perfumed oils, cosmetics, myrrh, cassia, frankincense with the curiously shaped spoons, the brilliantly polished brass mirrors with an ivory handle in the shape of the cow-headed goddess Hator.

Closing the procession came the kitchen utensils made of brass, the pots and pans, the large kettles and caldrons where the geese and meat joints will be prepared, the tubs where the dough will be kneaded, the presses to crush the juicy grapes and prepare wine.

The pageant went all over the town of Khut-

Aton through the narrow streets, giving to the public an exhibit of all the belongings of the bride, in order to show that her future husband was wealthy and generous and had lavishly furnished his home with all the luxury befitting the daughter of the reigning Pharaoh.

Another procession included the bridegroom, who rode in one of his chariots, with his tame lion sitting beside him, preceded by acrobats, mountebanks and wrestlers showing their skill. They were followed by his friends and servants walking on foot, singing his praise, and extolling to the skies his valor, and his qualities. They were very careful not to meet the cortege of the bride on the streets of the city and to reach the house before it in order to be ready to receive the princess.

The arrival of the princess at the house was announced by the piercing guttural shrills of the women. She was led to the presence of the bridegroom to whom she sang the following:

"*Thou hast called me to thee, Oh my Lord, and from the desert of my heart, I have heard thy voice, sweeter to my ear than the murmur of the Nile.*

"*I have answered thy call as the undaunted mare answers the call of the stallion, impatient to join her master.*

"*My soul was a thirsty caravan crossing*

the desert in search of the refreshing spring, and thou wilst quench my desire for thee.

"In the night of my solitude I was cold and thou wilst, Oh my Ra, Oh my sun, vivify my numb limbs.
"I have come to thee! I have come to thee!"

Tut-Ankh-Aton, enticed by her charm, answered:

"During my weary nights I have dreamt of thee, Oh fair Princess. I have called thee and thou hast come to me as a gift from the gods.
"Aton enlightens the villages of Egypt as thou enlighteneth my lonely life.
"Thou comst to me loftier than the palm tree, more gracile than the gazelle, lighter than the cool zephyrs of the North, bringing with thee the fragrance of the perfumes of Mitani.
"I will drink on thy lips the thrills of life, and to be happy will need no more wine.
"Come to me! I love thee! I love thee!"

Then the prepared feast started in the Banquet Hall, while the dancers were introduced to entertain the guests.

Tut-Ankh-Aton had built for her a magnificent palace on the outskirts of the city. Two pylons on which were inscribed magic formulae welcoming the stranger, and asking that no evil spirit be allowed to pass this barrier, flanked each side of the door. An alley of palm trees led to the house itself where quarters had been reserved for the princess and her suite. His own private apartments were near the door where he could entertain his friends, transact his business, receive the daily reports of his overseers and the manager of his vast estates. In the garden, lakes of refreshing water communicating directly with the Nile, had been prepared, where he could enjoy the pleasure of fishing, while his wife reposed leisurely under the shadows of the trees during the hot hours of the summer, or navigated with him in the sumptuous bark.

Akhen-Aton had bestowed upon him honors befitting to his rank and had nominated him Prince of Hermonthis, title which he kept when he became Pharaoh, and which brought with it the governorship of the southern part of Egypt. He was also appointed Royal Fan-bearer and general of the corps of archers, an honorary title, as Akhen-Aton hated blood-shed, and, unlike his predecessors, was not a warrior.

After his marriage, Tut-Ankh-Aton led the easy life of a nobleman and courtier. His functions were few besides attending the ceremonies and festivities of the royal palace.

Shortly afterwards, Akhen-Aton died, and his

second daughter with her husband, Saaka-Ra, succeeded him on the throne of Egypt.

The priests of Amon strenuously opposed the new Pharaoh because Saaka-Ra continued the policy of his predecessor, and the cult of "Aton." Tut-Ankh-Aton, approached, expressed his willingness to return to the faith of his fathers, abjure the heresy of Akhen-Aton, and abandon the city of Khut-Aton for Thebes, the old seat of the empire. Saaka-Ra, therefore, after a reign of a few months, was deposed or had to abdicate, to be succeeded by his brother-in-law. It is not known exactly how long he reigned, nor how he left the throne, as no traces of his disappearance and death were recorded on the monuments.

Tut-Ankh-Aton changed his name which means "the living image of Aton," into Tut-Ankh-Amen, and his wife, the own daughter of Akhen-Aton, changed her name from Ankh-Sen-Aton, which means "her life is from Aton" into Ankh-Sen-Amen to please the powerful priesthood. According to the tablet found by the late G. Legrain in 1905 in the ruins of the temple of Karanak, and now in the Cairo Museum, he was addressed thus: "Valiant Bull, image of birth, Lord of the Vulture and of the Uroeus, Excellent and Pacifier of the double country, Falcon of Gold, Offspring of the two diadems, Appeaser of the Gods, King of Upper and Lower Egypt, Son of the Sun, beloved of Amen-Ra, Lord of the thrones of the Two Lands, residing at **Thebes**, of Tum, lord of the Two Lands and of Heliopolis, of Ra-Hor-Akhuti, of Ptah-ra-sa-irab-eb, Living two Lands, Thot, lord of the Word of the Gods, who raiseth himself to the throne of Horus of the Living like his father, Ra, every day."

The investiture of Tut-Ankh-Amen took place at Karnak itself where he went in great pomp and was received by "Ay" the grand priest of Amen, who had married the nurse of Queen Thyi, wife of Amenhotep III and mother of Akhen-Aton. The ceremony took place in the temple of Amen at Karnak and in one of the sanctuaries where the Pharaoh was the only one allowed to enter. In this sanctuary he was left alone, changed his robes and put on the consecrated ones which he had to wear in the exercise of his functions, the long robes of linen braided with threads of gold and silver, the sandals turned at the toes, the gold uroeus sign of power, the double crown of the two lands, the red one of Lower Egypt, and the white cap of Upper Egypt.

By his communion with the Gods he acquired their omnipotence, and learned their hidden name so as to be able to call them when necessary and bid them to do what he ordered. He also learned the magic words which were supposed to give him power over the elements, and of raising the dead and talking with them.

The Pharaohs were not believed to be the actual descendants of the gods, and on no monuments is this descendance shown, as in the Greek history where some families pretended to descend from some demi-gods who had lived on earth at a certain period. The rulers represented on earth the Gods whose powers and attributes were bestowed upon them with their ascension on the throne; they were addressed as a personification of the Gods and their equal. These qualities were acquired, however, by their exalted position. The divine influence on their birth, as expressed in the temple of Amenhotep III at Karnak, and later in some temples of the Ptolemaic and Roman periods, seem to be more symbolical than a representation of actual facts. The Pharaohs were honored as the living image of the gods, having their authority over humans and their control over the elements.

Those who approached them did so with the greatest mark of respect, and it was considered good taste for a courtier to say he was blinded by the sight of the Pharaoh, as by the rays of the sun. In a letter, a nobleman boasted of having been allowed to kiss the feet of the King, instead of the ground on which he walked.

The reign of Tut-Ankh-Amen was not a quiet one; he had to contend with the turbulence and growing influence of the priests of Amen who had nominated him, and with the revolt of the conquered people who had been neglected during the reign of Akhen-Aton. He nominated Huy Viceroy of the South, and commissioned him to subjugate the restless tribes of the South and West, who had become obnoxious by their incursions in Egyptian territory.

He gave Huy his own ring, thus conferring on him his own power, and allowing him to seal the documents and issue decrees in his name. (This ring is actually in the Metropolitan Museum of New York). The Bible says that when Joseph became grand vizier of Egypt he was given the ring of the Pharaoh as a sign of authority.

We do not know if Tut-Ankh-Amen himself went to war, but certainly under his reign his armies went to Asia and tried to restore to the Empire its power and wealth. The general of the North was Horem-Heb, who later became a Pharaoh.

The strength of Egypt at that period was due to the discipline of the troops who knew how to march in ranks and thus defeat the undisciplined hordes of Asiatics. The Romans later adopted this formation in phalanxes and conquered the world. The superiority of Egyptians was also due to the great number of their horse-drawn chariots and to the skill of their archers who used flint or brass headed arrows.

Sometimes tame lions and leopards followed them in the wars, and fought side by side with them, throwing terror into the heart of their enemy.

To be skillful at war, was a great honor, which was rewarded by the granting of a golden collar as an insignia, just as today a medal or a cross is given to the soldier who has distinguished himself. Ahmone, son of Ebana, whose father Baba served under Sekenewre, says on his monument: "I followed the King on foot when he rode abroad in his chariot. I showed valor on foot before His Majesty, fought hand to hand, brought a hand as a trophy, reported it to His Majesty. "One" (the Pharaoh) gave me the gold of bravery."

At Thebes, Tut-Ankh-Amen, occupied the palace built by Amenhotep III on the Western bank of the Nile, and which an expedition of the Metropolitan Museum is excavating now. In the large halls, seated on a new throne with Amen designs, he gave audiences to the foreign embassadors, received the tributes of the vassals, and the offerings of his subjects, and of the 49 nomes or divisions of Egypt. As Pharaoh he was the owner of all the land, the taxes and tithes were due to him, and he used them for the different temples, the public works, and the maintenance of the army. He also held there a court of justice to try the most important cases, the minor ones going to the cheikh-el-balads, and the governors of the nomes. His decisions were without appeal.

These occupations and the daily ceremonies in the temple to keep in close touch with the Gods filled his time.

Under his reign, the cult of Amen was restored, the influence of the priests grew again, the wealth of the temples returned, and Aton was completely abandoned. New statues of Amen were erected and put in place. All this work was too much for the young king and he died after a few years.

Sir G. Maspero, late Director General of the Service of Antiquities in Egypt, believes that Tut-Ankh-Amen was consumptive and died from this terrible disease. Comparing the two statues of the God Khonsu and of Tut-Ankh-Amen, made at the same period, which are in the Cairo Museum, Sir G. Maspero says: "I think it evident they are by the same hand; the hollow of the eye is of the same depth in each; the line of the nose is identical, as are the hot inflation of the nostrils, the pout of the lips and the constriction of the corners of the mouth. The expression of suffering is common to both faces, but the indication of ill health, the hollow of the eyes, the thinness of the cheeks and neck, and the projecting shoulder blades are more marked in the Khonsu than in the Tut-Ankh-Amen: they betray consumptive tendencies which the artist has noticed with sufficient realism to enable the modern physician to diagnose the disease."

It also seems that Tut-Ankh-Amen was entirely under the influence of the high priest of Amen, and I would not be surprised if it were discovered that his death was hastened by the Amen priests when they noticed they were losing their influence upon him, but such actions are never discovered by history, they are just suspected. What leads me to such a conclusion, is the fact that after his death, his wife tried vainly to get rid of the Amen priests' rule and to marry a prince consort from Syria, but being unsuccessful, disappeared shortly after the death of her husband, to be succeeded by Ay, the hight priest of Amen during Tut-Ankh-Amen's reign.

The Queen widow, when left alone on the throne, wrote to the King of Mitani a touching letter, asking him to send one of his sons to become her husband, and the Pharaoh of Egypt, reminding him that her mother and grandmother were of his family. We do not know why her demand was refused and why she suddenly disappeared and was succeeded by the grand priest Ay.

The reign of Ay was of short duration and he was overthrown shortly after his ascension by Horem-Heb, general of the armies, who is said to have started the Pharaohs of the XIX Dynasty and the line of the Rameses.

SIGNIFICANCE OF THE TOMB

CHAPTER VI

SIGNIFICANCE OF THE TOMB

To understand the importance of the actual discovery made by Lord Carnarvon and Howard Carter's excavations, we must know the importance Egyptians attached to a proper burial, and their belief that the ultimate abode of the dead was part of his eternal dwelling in the underworld. His happiness would be measured by the means which would be afforded to him by the living to partake in peace of all the pleasures which he had enjoyed during life.

The tomb was not a mere cache in which all the treasures of the dead Pharaohs were piled up, but their real abode where personal belongings were gathered. Probably in this particular case, however, the fact that Tut-Ankh-Amen's widow was uncertain of her own future and feared the intrusion of a foreign ruler, prompted her to mass in the tomb all the Pharaoh's treasures in order they might not fall into foreign hands, feeling they were perfectly safe in the tomb against foreign intrusion. The popular belief at the time was so strong that anyone entering a tomb and appropriating any of the belongings was liable to immediate death besides being considered impure. Warnings were written at the entrance of the tomb saying: "As for any man who shall enter into this tomb, as his mortuary possession, I will seize him like a wild fowl: he shall be judged for it by the great God."

The story is related of an archeologist who found the mummy of a high priest, and when he started unwrapping it, read the following hieratic inscription: "The hand which dares to spoil my form will be immediately annihilated; crushed and scattered will be the bones of those who desecrate my body, my images and the effigies of my ka. The noble Ureus which crowns my brow will vomit annihilation on their head and everything will disappear of them, their ka, their ba and their khou." The archaeologist heedless of the warning unwrapped the mummy. A few months later while hunting big game in the Sudan, he was attacked by a mad elephant and trodden under its feet in the swamps with such rage that no traces of his body were ever found.

Of course, this did not prevent the tomb plunderers, who started as far back as 2000 B. C. to rob the tombs of their valuable belongings, and hardly a Pharaoh's tomb has ever been found which had not been tampered with. The profession of tomb thieves was very flourishing during

SIGNIFICANCE OF THE TOMB

all ages, at first for the gold, precious stones and ornaments which could be disposed of, then in the middle ages for the use of the Mummies' bodies as medicines. A brisk trade in what was called "mummies powder," a panacea for all ailments, took place all over Europe during the middle ages, and when the supply of mummies became scarce, fake mummies had to be made by the merchants of slaves' bodies to supply the demand.

During the modern times, the archaeologists' and tourists' demand for scarabs and antiques made the profession of tomb thieves very profitable. It is therefore most interesting for the archaeological world to find a tomb which had not been touched for the last 3000 years, and the actual seals of the Rameses inspector found on it.

A very interesting papyrus has been found relating to the finding of the robber who entered the tomb during Rameses III reign, his trial, his confession of the robbery, his condemnation and his final execution, when his body was torn in two.

We must not, however, place only on the robbers the responsibility of the ruins of all the monuments built in Egypt. The continual changes of power and of religions, which succeeded one another, are mainly responsible for the demolition of the temples and places of worship so numerous in the country. The iconoclasts with the establishment of the Christian religion, during the third and fourth centuries, as well as the Mahomedans, made it a point not to leave a statue unbroken or a temple standing.

From the most remote age, Egyptians built tombs to stay and always on the edge of the desert in the dry sand with its wonderful preserving qualities, where the water of the Nile could not reach and rot the remains. They were first oval mounds scarcely noticeable, then came the "mastabas," rectangular buildings resembling a truncated pyramid and divided mainly in three parts, the offering room or chapel, the shaft and the mortuary chambers. The pyramids followed this period, and later, tombs were hewn in the rock on the cliffs of the Lybian mountains, west of the Nile where the same distribution of rooms was kept, as in the primitive tombs. The shaft only changed into a more or less elongated sloping tunnel, entering into the heart of the mountain where the rooms were located.

The priests during the XVIII Dynasty owned all the slopes of the western hills at Thebes and built tombs which they sold to the faithfuls; the decorations, low reliefs, and paintings were ready. The name of the occupant was filled after the purchase. The cliff was honeycombed with tombs of all sizes and descriptions from the tomb of Seti I, which is 450 feet deep, to the tomb of Sekera, which is only one room.

The Pharaohs built their tombs during their life-time and, if they were not completed at the time of their death, the walls which ought to have been engraved were hastily painted and made ready during the period of the mummification. On the walls the mighty actions of the Pharaoh were reproduced; thus we know that Amenhotep III, the great hunter, killed 103 lions during ten years, that Thoutmes IV conquered many a country. If, as in the case of Tut-Ankh-Amen, the Pharaoh had died too young to have been to war, imaginary battles were depicted in which he was always victorious, and conquered nations were shown bringing tributes from every part of the world.

Also on the walls was depicted the voyage of the dead Pharaoh in the boat of the sun through the twelve divisions of the under-world, representing the twelve hours of the night, according to the ritual adopted through centuries in the "Book of the Dead." While passing in front of the principal gods he was either helped by some of them like Isis, Nephtys and Horus, or stopped by others like Set, the God of Evil, and different monsters, until he reached Osiris at the head of forty-two assessors sitting to judge the deeds of the newcomer, and where his heart was weighed against the feather of truth under the protection of Anubis, the jackal-headed god, protector of the dead, and Toth, the ibis headed god, protector of the scribes. Triumphant over darkness, serpents, and over all the dangers strewn in his path, the Pharaoh arrived at the twelfth hour to his father Amen-Ra, whose throne he shared and with whom he rode in the glory of the sun chariot.

Precautions were always taken to keep the location of the tomb known only to the priests who took care of its maintenance and the sacrifices. Robbers who may have found entrance to the tomb were fooled by finding wells dug in the main shafts and false corridors leading to blind doors. This is why so many tombs have not yet been located, and why even the entrances to the Pyramids have been discovered only during the past century.

The Pharaohs wanted to rest undisturbed in their tomb because from the earliest antiquity they knew that death did not mean end, but that man is composed of a body, a soul or "ba" and a double or "ka," and believed this immortal ka to occupy and literally live in the tomb.

What is a "ka"? No exact explanation has yet been given of a "ka," and to perfectly grasp the meaning of the word, we need the same power of abstraction acquired by this ancient people, for whom a privileged cast of priests had been thinking and studying for years. Ancient Egyptians had a knowledge of supernatural and astrology which has been lost and so far unattained by modern men. I do not agree with those who say that "their views were not the studied

SIGNIFICANCE OF THE TOMB 89

product of a highly trained mind and long developed self-consciousness; and on the contrary we have in them the involuntary and unconscious impressions of an early people."

It is again a case where an expression of an attribute is mistaken for the belief itself. The Egyptian religion was one of symbols and in honoring the "ka" under the form of a statue or a mummified body, Egyptians were only expressing as best they could their belief in the "principle of life, or the capability of giving life," as an immortal quality acquired with birth, but not extinct with death, and still existing after death in conjunction with the "soul" or "ba."

The nearest comprehension of this idea is what modern theosophists and spiritists call "astral body." They believe that our astral body can sometimes be separated from our mortal body, and does not die with it, but can come back to earth, having, however, lost its physical power, and manifest itself to those whose faculties are developed enough to be able to see it.

The Orientals believe actually that at birth the double of a man is born, invisible and intangible, leaving no shadows, but will accompany him everywhere and protect him.

This was the "ka," who did not die and for whom a royal tomb was prepared.

The "ka" who was shut in the tomb was supposed to live there with the needs and desires of a human body, going out when he wanted through a false door prepared for him; he needed therefore, all the furniture, the perfumes, the wines, the food, he used during his life.

Ancient Egyptians believed firmly that the "ka" was alive and was in close contact with the living. A very curious story, told in an ancient papyrus, has come down to us: It is the record of a suit brought by a widower against the "ka" of his wife. He complained to the proper tribunal of priests of the continual tribulations he suffered through the pursuit of this "ka." The poor man claimed that he had done everything in accordance with the law to honor his dead wife, and provide for her tomb; these provisions unavailing, he asked the priests to prevent, by words of magic, the "ka" of his wife from returning to the surface of earth,—one would call it an "injunction" in America. He probably had suffered enough from her during her lifetime. This reminds me of the curious suits brought in the sixteenth century by the inhabitants of some regions against dumb animals, like rats, locusts or cockroaches. The clergy was asked to exorcise these pests and order them out of the country.

This idea of "ka" was generalized and all things animated or unanimated were supposed to have a "ka"; and a "ka" for its sustenance and pleasure needed only the "ka" of other substances. One's servants would be the "ka" of one's life

SIGNIFICANCE OF THE TOMB 91

servants, and were represented by little statues called "Ushibiti," who would respond at one's call and work.

Tut-Ankh-Amen, following the example of his predecessors and the popular belief, had stored in his tomb the furniture, the robes, the garments, the chariots which he had used during his life. His favorite dishes were mummified, the choice wines and beers from his cellars, the preferred perfumes, and the best unguents were gathered ready for his use.

As this accumulation could run short in an endless life, the daily activities were reproduced on the walls of the tombs, and the "ka" was shown directing the work of his servants who were sowing, harvesting, winnowing, picking grapes, kneading dough, baking bread, preparing wine and beer, slaughtering cattle, so that in case of need the "ka" would order his servants' "ka" to work for him as they used to during his life. He had thus an inexhaustible and always renewable supply.

These preparations were done during the life of the Pharaoh, and part of the furniture gathered there was furniture used long before his death. This is why in Tut-Ankh-Amen's tomb we find a throne with an Aton design on it and belonging certainly to the first period of his reign. When he changed his former belief and returned to the Amen faith, he probably stored this throne in his tomb, as it was too good a work of art to be destroyed. In a papyrus, a prince called Sinuhit, living during the XII Dynasty, tells how he prepared his tomb before his death and says: "All kinds of furnishing were placed in the storehouses (of the tomb) and all that was needful was placed there . . . I gave the furniture, making the necessary arrangements in the pyramid itself."

This explains why such a variety of furnishing and clothing is found in the tombs. Accumulated there was everything which had been used during the dead man's life, even dolls and toys of his childhood, as is found in many a tomb of grown up.

Tut-Ankh-Amen, besides storing in his tomb the necessities for the sustenance of his "ka," had, following the habit of his predecessors, richly endowed his tomb and affected for its maintenance the revenues of some lands and tributes paid by conquered countries. In a decree he had set fixed days of general festivities during which public distribution of bread, geese and wine were to be made to the people in his honor.

Many of these customs have remained popular through centuries and now after thousands of years we see the same habits recurring in Egypt. Many modern Egyptians in their wills entail part or all of their revenues to provide bread and food for the poor after their death, to be distributed on their tombs. This is known as "Wakf."

Most of the modern cemeteries are on the west side of the Nile. Regular houses are built for the dead, and in them are enclosed their tombs. The descendants and relatives of the deceased gather in these houses once a year, live there for two or three days, cooking and eating, believing that they are thus in closer contact and direct communion with the dear departed one, whose "double" comes back and lives with them during this short period, grateful of the marks of attention paid to him.

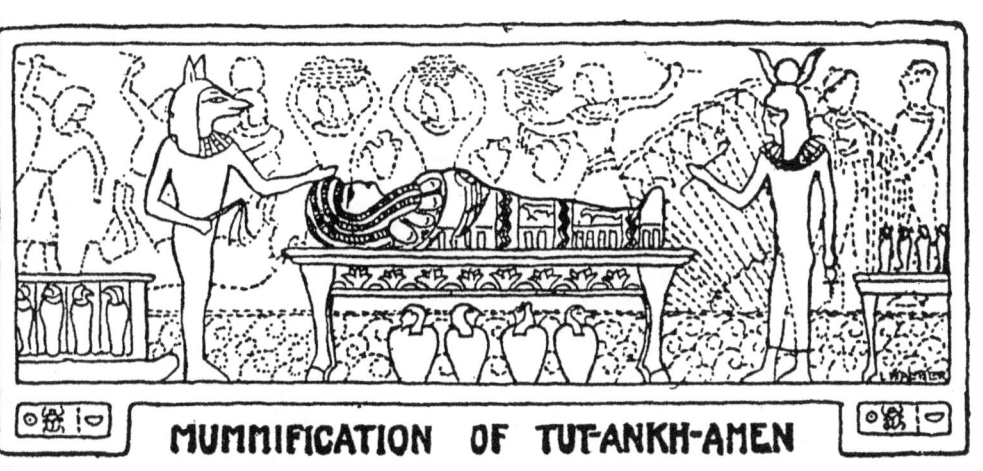

CHAPTER VII

MUMMIFICATION OF TUT-ANKH-AMEN

To understand better the symbols of the Pharaoh's burial, let us go back 3300 years and visualize the funeral as it actually took place.

Some customs have remained unchanged and for an Egyptian who has lived there, and knows the habits of the country, it is possible to see the manifestation of the same ceremonies which have gone unbroken through centuries in the same climate and under the same sun.

As soon as the news of the Pharaoh's death reached the population, all the inhabitants wept, tore their garments and showed external signs of grief and sorrow. Crowds of men and women went about the streets with mud on their head, singing and wailing. Diodorus of Sicily tells us, "the temples were closed and no festivals were celebrated for a period of seventy-two days until the body was mummified. People would not make use of baths, or perfume, abstained from eating meat or fish, and drinking wine. They even denied themselves the pleasures of love."

The priests in charge of the embalming took possession of the body and started immediately to prepare it according to the ritual established by thousands of years practice. They carried it in the embalming chamber of the temple of "Amon-Ra" at Karnak, and laid it on the embalming stone where it was washed religiously. A corrosive was injected into the brain to soften its contents, which were then drawn out through the nostrils by means of a hooked piece of iron. The process was done carefully so as not to break the nasal arch, then with red ink, the assistant to the high priest marked on the left side a line which indicated where an incision was to be made to take out the internal membranes of the body. The lowest one in the cast, a pariah amongst the priests, made the incision with a flint knife. Immediately after having done so, struck by the enormity of his action, he would run away as if followed by the revengeful spirit of the dead, because a dead body was such a sacred thing to the ancient Egyptians.

The intestines, stomach, lungs and heart, the liver and gall bladder were taken out, carefully washed, smeared with unguent and stuffed with spices. They were then bandaged with strips of linen and carefully placed in four jars, each dedicated to one of the sons of Horus, the cover of each jar representing the head of each deity. The stomach and large intestines were placed in the jar of Masti, the man-headed; the small intestines in the jar of Hapi, the dog-headed; the lungs and heart in the jar of Tutmutef, the jakal-headed; and the liver and gall bladder in the jar of Quebksennuf, the hawk-headed. On each jar the Cartouche of Tut-Ankh-Amen with all his titles was inscribed.

Then the body underwent a drying process. It was stripped of all its flesh with the skin remaining only on the bone. To give it its natural form, it was skillfully stuffed with sawdust mixed with myrrh, cassia, cedar oil and spices. It was then sewed and soaked in a brine of natron for seventy days. Natron, which is a carbonate and muriate of soda, is found in very large quantities in the Egyptian desert. After the period of seventy days, the body was taken out, carefully washed, the nails stained with henna, the skull cavity filled with natron and spices, and the nostrils plugged with strips of linen. The body had then acquired a brownish gray color and thus would last for eternity.

The washing of the body was followed by the process of bandaging in which thousands of yards of very fine linen, cut in strips, dipped in adhesive substance, were used. Between the bandages were inserted scrolls of papyrus containing extracts from the Book of the Dead. During his lifetime, Tut-Ankh-Amen, as High Priest of Amon, was well versed in all knowledge of magic. He knew exactly how to fight the evil spirits who would prevent him from joining his father Amen-Ra after his traveling in the underworld, but in spite of the knowledge he had acquired, this papyrus on which magic formulae were written would help him through his tenebrous journey.

Nothing was left to uncertainty, and if his memory failed he would find in the papyrus the words of magic which would open the closed doors and chase away the evils and serpents he would meet. One of the papyrus contained the famous confession of forty-two negations, one for each assessor sitting with Osiris in the final tribunal, which he had to recite, saying: "There was no peasant whom I evicted, no widow whom I afflicted. I have not been the cause of others' tears. I have not caught fish by bait of fishes' body. I have not taken away the cakes of the child, etc. . . . etc. I am pure! I am pure! I am pure!"

The terms of this so-called negative confession show the high standard of morality of the Egyptians of three thousand years ago. Anyone following their principles today would be considered an upright man well deserving of the honor of the community. While on earth they prepared themselves to die, and their ambition was to lead during this mortal and transitory period a life which would make them worthy of sharing the throne with Amen-Ra.

On the small finger of Tut-Ankh-Amen's left hand was his golden ring, in which was set a scarab, emblem of revivification, and on his breast was laid a large green basalt scarab, mounted on solid gold, on which his name was inscribed and under the name a prayer saying: "Oh, my heart, rise not up against me as a witness." This prayer would prevent his heart when weighed on the balance against the feather of truth from saying anything against him.

This was, of course, the most expensive way of mummifying the body, there were several other methods reported by Herodotus and Diodorus of Sicily. The second one was by the injection of cedar oil in the body before dipping it in the natron bath. After a period of seventy days the body was taken out and emptied from its cedar oil, which brought out with it all the internal organs. A third method was of dipping the body in a bath of natron without the cedar oil. It is very pobable that the poorer classes contented themselves with a simple drying in the sun if they could not afford the price of a regular mummification.

In the later periods the body was dipped in bitumen instead of natron, and the word "mummy" which means bitumen in Arabic comes from this habit. Honey was used sometimes and it is said that the body of Alexander the Great was preserved in honey. An Arabic writer speaks of his adventure when he found a jar which he broke and found full of honey, his companions and himself dipped their bread in it, and ate some before noticing that the jar contained the body of a young boy.

CHAPTER VIII

FUNERAL FESTIVITIES

The process of mummification having been completed, the tomb was ready, and as there was not time enough to sculpture in bas-relief all the scenes on the walls, they had been drawn in vivid colors made to last forever. The carpenters had also finished the beautifully carved coffins made to measure from sycamore wood which never rots. The outer cover in the form of Osiris, but whose face resembled Tut-Ankh-Amen's, fitted exactly the body which was placed in an inner coffin, in the form of a mummy. Its bottom and sides were made of one piece and fastened together with wooden pegs. Inside there was a wooden pillow or "urs" to lift up the head of the mummy.

The goddess Isis and Nephtys were handsomely painted at each end of the coffin, kneeling in protection of the dead, Anubis, the jackal-headed god who presides over the funeral, was painted on the top. The coffin was ornamented with inscriptions bearing the name of the Pharaoh, his titles, and praising his actions. The inner coffin was contained in an outer one made on the same shape and model as the first.

The mourning and fasting of the people had ceased by now as they were informed that the Pharaoh was ready to be carried to his tomb. He was no more referred to as being dead, but was called "Osiris," and the people prepared for the great festivities accompanying the transportation of the body to the other side of the Nile.

The body in its coffins had been brought in great procession from the temple of Karnak to the temple of Amon-Ra at Luxor, through the broad and magnificent avenue boarded by sphynxes on the two sides, and was lying in the sanctuary of the temple.

In the outer parts of the temple, during his life, Tut-Ankh-Amen had completed the building started by his predecessor Amenhotep III, and had built a wide hall sustained by a double row of eight columns each. On the walls he had represented the festivities held during the feast of Amen in the Apts. Later his successor, Horemneb, was going to add his own cartouche (name of the Pharaoh in a seal), to the cartouche of Tut-Ankh-Amen in order to usurp his rights to have erected this temple to Amon.

The festivities in honor of the transportation of the mummy from Karnak to Thebes were held as represented on the walls of the temple.

Twelve girls, castanets in hands, covered with

lovely white veils, danced the sacred dance, moving gracefully and bending themselves in ecstasy till their hands touched the ground behind them. Eight girls play the sistrum and shake the timbrel while the blind musicians attached to the temple accompanied them with the harp and the "darabouka." Twelve girls sang in a low melodious voice dirges in honor of the deceased, praising his virtues, saying:

> *"Come to thy temple, come to thy temple, Oh Beautiful youth, immediately, immediately. . . . We see thee not, our heart is full of sorrow, our eyes search for thee. . . . Oh Osiris . . . We are near thee by thy bier, and we cry to thee shading tears. Look thou at thy fair women who love thee, speak to us, Oh King, our Lord . . . Destroy the sorrow which is in our hearts . . . Our faces live in seeing thy face, our hearts will rejoice at the sight of thee, Oh Beautiful King. Oh Powerful . . . We seek to see thee because of our love for thee. Come to us in thine own form, come in peace, Oh King of the two Lands . . . At the sight of thee thy enemies will flee."*

In the meantime the priests poured wine into tall jars, which were going to be stored in the tombs. All the offerings were gathered, the sacred barques, the vases, the chests containing the Pharaoh's robes, innumerable "ushibiti" statuettes of servants, and amulets by the thousands as: red buckles representing the rejuvenating blood of Isis, collars of gold in the shape of a diadem, signs of wealth, papyrus sceptres indicating eternal youth, vultures asking Isis to be propitious, Osiris plumes to ask this god's protection, "urst" pillows to lift up and raise up the mummy, disks of the orbit of the sun in its full course, and of the setting sun, red and white crowns of lower and upper Egypt signs of power, stairs to help the deceased to go high up to the sky, serpents' heads to protect from snake bites, frogs representing myriads of years of life, two fingers, the index and medius superposed, protection against the evil eyes.

They were consecrated and blest by aspersion with holy water from the libation vases; so were the flowers and fruits which were to be borne in the procession.

During this time the population was not allowed in the temple, but massed on the outside where it could hear the music and the voices of the singers, impatiently waited for the opening of the "very great double doors of electrum (alloy of gold and silver), of which beauty met the heavens."

The body was then taken on the State boat, of which the rostrum was all gold plated, the masts were of cedar and precious woods, and the sails of the finest purple linen. In solemnity the Nile was crossed to take the Pharaoh on the western bank where his tomb had been prepared, high up under the cliff, in this desolate part of the country where he will rest in eternal peace. From there the view commands a large portion of the Nile and of the rich valleys of Egypt upon which he once reigned, an undisturbed ruler.

On the western bank the procession proper formed itself, a procession much similar to one of today's, as the Egyptians have kept the custom of burying their dead on the west side at the edge of the desert, and of accompanying them ceremoniously to their last abode.

Opening the march were the poor and blind and miserable wailing and lamenting because they had lost a father and a purveyor.

Next came the bearers of the funeral offerings, the mummified food, the chests, the amulets, the furniture and the royal chairs from the palace, all the furniture bearing the seal of Tut-Ankh-Amen, or the reproduction of his portraits and his wife's in gold inlaid with semi-precious stones. His thrones, his chariots, his beds, his weapons and insignia were there. His successor was supposed to have new furniture made bearing his own cartouche. Tut-Ankh-Amen was wealthy and powerful and the procession of bearers was endless.

After them came the priests bearing the attributes of the god whom they served, and in order of their importance. They were divided in seven classes, each class recognizable by the color and material of their garments. The last carried on their shoulders the golden barque with oars of gold on which Tut-Ankh-Amen was to travel in the underworld. The High Priest came after them wearing a panther skin, insignia of his rank.

He directly preceded the catafalque drawn by four pairs of oxen and on which was the coffin under a double canopy of gold cloth, the four posts of which were the four gods of the four cardinal points. At the head of the coffin is a figure of Nepthys and at the foot a figure of Isis, both praying and assuring the Pharaoh of their protection. Kneeling besides the coffin was the Queen Ankh-Sen-Amen, her hair spread on her shoulders, her breast naked, having the marks of the deepest sorrow. Perfidious Queen, who was already corresponding with some foreign prince to marry him and bring him on the throne of Egypt, left vacant by the deceased, whom she affected to regret so deeply!

After the coffin and under another canopy was a chest surmounted by Anubis, the jackal-headed god, in which were the four jars containing the viscera of the deceased. The posts of this canopy represented the four sons of Horus like the jars.

Following them came the official mourners, who still in modern Egypt follow the funeral procession and are dressed as centuries ago: a deep purple band around their head, wearing flowing robes, they have in one hand a long veil which they agitate in the air while they lament loudly, and in the other hand a pear shaped lacrymatory vase in which they gather their tears. They gnash their teeth, beat their uncovered breasts in the expression of deepest sorrow. The rhythm of their lamentation is unknown, but I would not be surprised if it would be the same long wail heard today when they chant: "La Allah illa Allah."

Closing the procession came priests bearing incense burners, and flowers. Then all the population of Thebes followed.

The procession was so long that the head of it had reached the tomb six miles away, when the end was not even at half the distance, so when the body arrived, all the furniture and offerings were in place in the numerous chambers. The coffins were then brought in the tomb, set standing and uncovered for the operation of the "opening of the mouth." The process of mummification had deprived the deceased of the use of his faculties; to enable him to regain possession of them, the High Priest with a specially hooked iron stood in front of the mummy and opened its mouth saying the magic formula: "I open thy mouth with that instrument with which Ptah opened the mouth of the gods." Then the dead Pharaoh was again in possession of his faculties and could have intercourse with the gods.

The coffins were then sealed with plaster and placed in a magnificent alabaster sarcophagus under the canopies. Everyone present retired from the tomb, the priests carefully sealing the doors with magic words as they left, and hiding even the doors the best they could. The last door of the tomb was sealed and on it the following prayer was written: "O ye living who are upon earth, who shall pass by this tomb, whether going down stream or up stream, who shall say, 'A thousand loaves, a thousand jars of beer for the owner of this tomb.' I will intercede for their sake in the nether-world."

The belief in the immortality of man was deeply rooted in the souls of Tut-Ankh-Amen's contemporaries, as was their belief in the intimate and constant contact of the dead with the living, one assisting the other. As far as we can remember, man has tried to persuade himself that mortal life was not all, and Egyptians have made of future life the ultimate aim of our actual tribulations. Comforting thought which allowed them to say of their dead: "They depart not as those who are dead, but they depart as those who are living."

ORDER FROM YOUR FAVORITE BOOKSELLER OR CALL FOR OUR FREE CATALOG

Of Heaven and Earth: Essays Presented at the First Sitchin Studies Day, edited by Zecharia Sitchin. ISBN 1-885395-17-5 • 164 pages • 5 1/2 x 8 1/2 • trade paper • illustrated • $14.95

God Games: What Do You Do Forever?, by Neil Freer. ISBN 1-885395-39-6 • 312 pages • 6 x 9 • trade paper • $19.95

Space Travelers and the Genesis of the Human Form: Evidence of Intelligent Contact in the Solar System, by Joan d'Arc. ISBN 1-58509-127-8 • 208 pages • 6 x 9 • trade paper • illustrated • $18.95

Humanity's Extraterrestrial Origins: ET Influences on Humankind's Biological and Cultural Evolution, by Dr. Arthur David Horn with Lynette Mallory-Horn. ISBN 3-931652-31-9 • 373 pages • 6 x 9 • trade paper • $17.00

Past Shock: The Origin of Religion and Its Impact on the Human Soul, by Jack Barranger. ISBN 1-885395-08-6 • 126 pages • 6 x 9 • trade paper • illustrated • $12.95

Flying Serpents and Dragons: The Story of Mankind's Reptilian Past, by R.A. Boulay. ISBN 1-885395-38-8 • 276 pages • 6 x 9 • trade paper • illustrated • $19.95

Triumph of the Human Spirit: The Greatest Achievements of the Human Soul and How Its Power Can Change Your Life, by Paul Tice. ISBN 1-885395-57-4 • 295 pages • 6 x 9 • trade paper • illustrated • $19.95

Mysteries Explored: The Search for Human Origins, UFOs, and Religious Beginnings, by Jack Barranger and Paul Tice. ISBN 1-58509-101-4 • 104 pages • 6 x 9 • trade paper • $12.95

Mushrooms and Mankind: The Impact of Mushrooms on Human Consciousness and Religion, by James Arthur. ISBN 1-58509-151-0 • 180 pages • 6 x 9 • trade paper • $16.95

Vril or Vital Magnetism, with an Introduction by Paul Tice. ISBN 1-58509-030-1 • 124 pages • 5 1/2 x 8 1/2 • trade paper • $12.95

The Odic Force: Letters on Od and Magnetism, by Karl von Reichenbach. ISBN 1-58509-001-8 • 192 pages • 6 x 9 • trade paper • $15.95

The New Revelation: The Coming of a New Spiritual Paradigm, by Arthur Conan Doyle. ISBN 1-58509-220-7 • 124 pages • 6 x 9 • trade paper • $12.95

The Astral World: Its Scenes, Dwellers, and Phenomena, by Swami Panchadasi. ISBN 1-58509-071-9 • 104 pages • 6 x 9 • trade paper • $11.95

Reason and Belief: The Impact of Scientific Discovery on Religious and Spiritual Faith, by Sir Oliver Lodge. ISBN 1-58509-226-6 • 180 pages • 6 x 9 • trade paper • $17.95

William Blake: A Biography, by Basil De Selincourt. ISBN 1-58509-225-8 • 384 pages • 6 x 9 • trade paper • $28.95

The Divine Pymander: And Other Writings of Hermes Trismegistus, translated by John D. Chambers. ISBN 1-58509-046-8 • 196 pages • 6 x 9 • trade paper • $16.95

Theosophy and The Secret Doctrine, by Harriet L. Henderson. Includes *H.P. Blavatsky: An Outline of Her Life,* by Herbert Whyte, ISBN 1-58509-075-1 • 132 pages • 6 x 9 • trade paper • $13.95

The Light of Egypt, Volume One: The Science of the Soul and the Stars, by Thomas H. Burgoyne. ISBN 1-58509-051-4 • 320 pages • 6 x 9 • trade paper • illustrated • $24.95

The Light of Egypt, Volume Two: The Science of the Soul and the Stars, by Thomas H. Burgoyne. ISBN 1-58509-052-2 • 224 pages • 6 x 9 • trade paper • illustrated • $17.95

The Jumping Frog and 18 Other Stories: 19 Unforgettable Mark Twain Stories, by Mark Twain. ISBN 1-58509-200-2 • 128 pages • 6 x 9 • trade paper • $12.95

The Devil's Dictionary: A Guidebook for Cynics, by Ambrose Bierce. ISBN 1-58509-016-6 • 144 pages • 6 x 9 • trade paper • $12.95

The Smoky God: Or The Voyage to the Inner World, by Willis George Emerson. ISBN 1-58509-067-0 • 184 pages • 6 x 9 • trade paper • illustrated • $15.95

A Short History of the World, by H.G. Wells. ISBN 1-58509-211-8 • 320 pages • 6 x 9 • trade paper • $24.95

The Voyages and Discoveries of the Companions of Columbus, by Washington Irving. ISBN 1-58509-500-1 • 352 pages • 6 x 9 • hard cover • $39.95

History of Baalbek, by Michel Alouf. ISBN 1-58509-063-8 • 196 pages • 5 x 8 • trade paper • illustrated • $15.95

Ancient Egyptian Masonry: The Building Craft, by Sommers Clarke and R. Engelback. ISBN 1-58509-059-X • 350 pages • 6 x 9 • trade paper • illustrated • $26.95

That Old Time Religion: The Story of Religious Foundations, by Jordan Maxwell and Paul Tice. ISBN 1-58509-100-6 • 220 pages • 6 x 9 • trade paper • $19.95

Jumpin' Jehovah: Exposing the Atrocities of the Old Testament God, by Paul Tice. ISBN 1-58509-102-2 • 104 pages • 6 x 9 • trade paper • $12.95

The Book of Enoch: A Work of Visionary Revelation and Prophecy, Revealing Divine Secrets and Fantastic Information about Creation, Salvation, Heaven and Hell, translated by R. H. Charles. ISBN 1-58509-019-0 • 152 pages • 5 1/2 x 8 1/2 • trade paper • $13.95

The Book of Enoch: Translated from the Editor's Ethiopic Text and Edited with an Enlarged Introduction, Notes and Indexes, Together with a Reprint of the Greek Fragments, edited by R. H. Charles. ISBN 1-58509-080-8 • 448 pages • 6 x 9 • trade paper • $34.95

The Book of the Secrets of Enoch, translated from the Slavonic by W. R. Morfill. Edited, with Introduction and Notes by R. H. Charles. ISBN 1-58509-020-4 • 148 pages • 5 1/2 x 8 1/2 • trade paper • $13.95

Enuma Elish: The Seven Tablets of Creation, Volume One, by L. W. King. ISBN 1-58509-041-7 • 236 pages • 6 x 9 • trade paper • illustrated • $18.95

Enuma Elish: The Seven Tablets of Creation, Volume Two, by L. W. King. ISBN 1-58509-042-5 • 260 pages • 6 x 9 • trade paper • illustrated • $19.95

Enuma Elish, Volumes One and Two: The Seven Tablets of Creation, by L. W. King. Two volumes from above bound as one. ISBN 1-58509-043-3 • 496 pages • 6 x 9 • trade paper • illustrated • $38.90

The Archko Volume: Documents that Claim Proof to the Life, Death, and Resurrection of Christ, by Drs. McIntosh and Twyman. ISBN 1-58509-082-4 • 248 pages • 6 x 9 • trade paper • $20.95

The Lost Language of Symbolism: An Inquiry into the Origin of Certain Letters, Words, Names, Fairy-Tales, Folklore, and Mythologies, by Harold Bayley. ISBN 1-58509-070-0 • 384 pages • 6 x 9 • trade paper • $27.95

The Book of Jasher: A Suppressed Book that was Removed from the Bible, Referred to in Joshua and Second Samuel, translated by Albinus Alcuin (800 AD). ISBN 1-58509-081-6 • 304 pages • 6 x 9 • trade paper • $24.95

The Bible's Most Embarrassing Moments, with an Introduction by Paul Tice. ISBN 1-58509-025-5 • 172 pages • 5 x 8 • trade paper • $14.95

History of the Cross: The Pagan Origin and Idolatrous Adoption and Worship of the Image, by Henry Dana Ward. ISBN 1-58509-056-5 • 104 pages • 6 x 9 • trade paper • illustrated • $11.95

Was Jesus Influenced by Buddhism? A Comparative Study of the Lives and Thoughts of Gautama and Jesus, by Dwight Goddard. ISBN 1-58509-027-1 • 252 pages • 6 x 9 • trade paper • $19.95

History of the Christian Religion to the Year Two Hundred, by Charles B. Waite. ISBN 1-885395-15-9 • 556 pages • 6 x 9 • hard cover • $25.00

Symbols, Sex, and the Stars, by Ernest Busenbark. ISBN 1-885395-19-1 • 396 pages • 5 1/2 x 8 1/2 • trade paper • $22.95

History of the First Council of Nice: A World's Christian Convention, A.D. 325, by Dean Dudley. ISBN 1-58509-023-9 • 132 pages • 5 1/2 x 8 1/2 • trade paper • $12.95

The World's Sixteen Crucified Saviors, by Kersey Graves. ISBN 1-58509-018-2 • 436 pages • 5 1/2 x 8 1/2 • trade paper • $29.95

www.ingramcontent.com/pod-product-compliance
Lightning Source LLC
Chambersburg PA
CBHW031651040426
42453CB00006B/268